Voters' Guide to Recognizing Political Con-Games

Voters' Guide to Recognizing Political Con-Games

Robert Shelven

To order additional copies of this book, contact:
Xlibris LLC
1-888-795-4274
www.Xlibris.com
Orders@Xlibris.com
622328

Contents

Chapter One

THE ME-ME CANDIDATE

This type of candidate loves talking about themselves and or their families without sharing their plans and ideas on how to make our everyday lives better than what they are. With an attitude of trust me and elect-me!

Examples: Congress woman Michelle Bachman who talks about herself, her faith and her family and always criticizing liberals and other democrats. But don't like talking about issues and problems.

Or business I-con Donald Trump patting himself on the back he made the president show his birth certificate!

Like seeing them on T.V. when you mute the sound and you can hear them sing Me! Me! Me! Me! Me!

When what they really portray is arrogance and conceit.

Chapter Two

EARMARKS AND PORK BARRELS

And other Legislative blunders

The real definition of earmarks: Any proposal that has funding and or allotted money marked specific funding for a program and or agency which means that money has to be used specifically for that program and or Agency.

Examples: Educational programs or food or nutritional programs and or health programs all carry earmarks. For instance, Social Security, Medicare, Medicaid, and Food stamps.

Now in Congress and Senate they ban legislation with any earmarks in it. Now myself I would much rather have earmarks funding than have a notion that they can move Tax-Dollars around like a shell game. What shell is the money under?

Pork Barrels:

True definition: A program they feel cost a lot to have the program to fund it.

Examples: Defense Dept., Social Security, Medicare and Medicaid.

My opinion is they to control the cost-of-living or inflation instead of cutting budgets because we can't afford the cost of these programs. Even talking about privatizing these programs.

When they should end supply sides economics and let the American People have the government services they pay for. Everybody that lives in this country should pay their taxes so that everybody can have the government services they pay for.

I sometimes wonder what moderate-Democrats are thinking when they are always trying to make some kind of deal with conservatives, only to make the middle class tax payer hate the poor even more than they use to. One good example is the sequester cuts which actually total $85 billion dollars per month for seven months. When they promise to restore those cuts and turn-around and restore FAA funding because it affected government and Rich people air travel and all other cuts, Will go as they are! And you wonder whose side are they on!

Chapter Three

THE TAX & SPEND LIBERAL

Here are the people that are evil! And according to conservatives we append a whole lot of money in when we govern and we sin a lot, we are weak on defense of our country to keep us safe! And I know that a liberal can't be trusted to have any governance position regardless if it's dog catcher to yes president of United States. They are socialists and or Communists! Let alone un-American so conservatives have us to believe. OH! My Goodness! Damn! I almost forgot we are whiny & pouty sissy like cusses. And Bill O'Reilly with his portrayal and vivid description of Liberal pinheads!

Well how about another view!

Most of my life I have heard those principals and descriptions when actually we have either moderate democrats or republicans with the majorities either in state government or in the federal government. Liberals have never really have had much of a say in government policy except 2014. You can look it up in our history and I challenge anybody to know those facts. Not all democrats are liberal's people! Just remember that thought as you look that up to find out that information. I don't even consider President Franklin Roosevelt to be a liberal when he have signed the Marijuana tax stamp act of 1930 knowing that a Tax stamp never existed? Last but not Lease something for Bill O'Reilly I would rather be a liberal pinhead! Than be a *conservative—con-artist!*

Was President Clinton a Liberal? When he repealed the Glass-Steagle act that separated investment banks form commercial banks or free-trade agreement so that general motors could finally and legally move their Flint Michigan Plant to Mexico! NO! I don't believe a true liberal would have done that.

The only reason they're on T.V. & radio with their commentary was to try not to pay their fair share in taxes which I believe is un-American! They go to great lengths to protect current tax laws. A bit of Liberal American Philosophy.

If you live here, you have a business here then you can pay you're fair share of taxes, and abide by laws. If you don't you can go to jail just like me, if I don't abide by laws! Let's be fair.

Chapter Four

SYMPATHY SHUFFLE AND DESPERATION DIVE

The sympathy shuffle; the sympathy shuffle is when any candidate uses a disability or tragic Accident or illness of themselves or family members to get elected. Moderates and conservatives mostly use this con-game.

In the 2008 Presidential Election, Vice Presidential candidate Sarah Palin using her sons learning disability to try and help herself and presidential candidate John Midair until the News Media well publicized her budget cuts in learning disability programs in Alaska while she was Governor form Educational programs and refuse to fund the special Olympics.

Blamed in her words the Lame-stream news media! Lies! However; To this day these charges have never been proven wrong by Governor Palin.

Sympathy Shuffle is always designed to get you to feel sorry for the candidate to vote for them. And to show they have compassion to be cautious. Always pay attention to see how many times they tell that story if they tell it a lot it turns from one time story in to a shuffle, becoming repetitious to shuffle on.

Desperation Dive

It's like being in a plane up 150,000 ft. in the air and running out of gas so out of desperation you make up some story to increase poll numbers and to get new contributors and raise them poll numbers at all cost or crash & burn!

Examples: The 1980 Presidential election when President Carter Blew up National debt and deficit when there was no deficit or very small. When Presidential candidate Mitt Romney accused president Obama cutting Medicare Benefits by $750 Billion dollars.

Chapter Five

FLIP, FLOP, & FLY

Flip-Flop and Fly, Being in support for a program agency or cause one day, then being against it the very next day and be in support of the day after that almost like smacking a Ping-Pong ball back and forth—back and forth. Making it repetitious thus Flip—Flopping and Flying.

Perfect examples: Listening to Former Governor Mitt Romney Flip-Flopping so much I don't think anybody really knows what he is for or against creating distrust, except for more supply-side Economic programs.

Chapter Six

SUPPLY-SIDE ECONOMICS AND OTHER
ECONOMIC TALES:

Let's start with supply-side economics, Rich-people with extra money to tax credits that are supposed to spur-economic growth by creating jobs creating a trickle-down effect to grow the economy. And we will cut and cap Human-Services and Entitlements to help pay for those tax—credits.

Sound so good in theory and on paper that Former Congressman jack Kemp wrote a book about it, a supply-side Economy where there is no welfare or poverty but plenty of well salaried jobs & middle class wages. But let's talk about the true cause effect of this created with its high debt and deficits instead of its surpluses as well Tax increases on the middle-class.

Of course conservatives see the middle-class differently. To them income for middle class earners usually is $100,000 to about $300,000. Now middle class to me is $30,000 to $100,000 it used to be middle-class went by stages middle to Upper middle-class until it was they created tax indexing which made it easier to raise the Marginal Tax-Rate!

Now what I believe what makes it a con-game is when they campaign for their elections and re-elections with that Great-American White Lie: on their lips telling you how their goanna let you keep more of your money that you have worked so hard for. So goes supply-side Economics.

This is what I think!

"Tax—cuts for Job-creators" "Is legalized tax deductible campaign contributions"

Because the only jobs I have seen that's created is more registered Lobbyists or jobs that defeat Democrats and it's no Big conservative secret that the Bush tax cuts paid for the Tea-Party, and added 12 trillion Dollars to the National Debt! So moderates & conservatives where are the Jobs?

I am **OUTRAGED!** Over knowing that higher Marginal tax rates that has really upset the middle class for the last 35 years. Especially when more poverty is created and cannot be cleaned up anytime soon because they believe the working poor and the poverty stricken should be pushed to go to work without better pay to keep up with inflation and or cost of Living! If they push people to go to work, then push that corporate mogul to hire them with decent pay for a decent days work! Now let's have a decent discussion about the Economy! But remember the Nation's Economy has 9 different living parts to it.

1. Jobs & Unemployment
2. Inflation-cost of Living and Recession Bubbles
3. Taxes
4. Healthcare & Well Being
5. Education-Public schools and Higher Education (college)
6. Safety & Security
7. Climate Change
8. Measuring Gross Domestic Product (G.O.P.)
9. National Debt & Deficit

For the last thirty five years the American people have been laid off of their jobs and the reason that's giving is for economic reasons with less releases of a plant hut power but! You also don't know that they turn in a productivity report that is filled out and turned in every physical year, which is in quarter year, (approx., every four months.) Claiming a lack of productivity in their company which they can legally raise the price of their product and or services. *Ground zero* for *inflation*. Also we have not had a low unemployment rate and I believe they like a high unemployment rate. Just so they can have high-school graduates to enlist in the armed forces so they can fight the wars that they get into.

Because if you can't find a job you join the military! Use common sense here! Not only that, here is something else to think about, chairman of the federal reserve bank Ben Bernanke says he will not raise interest rates until the unemployment rate reaches 6.5%. Do you realize that when interest rates are raised our cost-of-living or inflation goes up! Prices on everything from bubble gum to gasoline, as well as services fees. When that happens I don't think that even a raise in minimum wages is going to make a difference.

1. Job's and Unemployment:

There was however in the 2012 Presidential Election the mention of employment problems by Republican candidate Mitt Romney, he briefly mentioned under employment. Part of the rigging of our society goes on with under-employment, but it does go deeper than that. I remember growing up when corporations hired directly off the street and paying above average wages to where you can get by and have your entertainment on your days off without putting yourself in debt over it or making yourself homeless over it! Until with no fault of their own they are laid off for economic reasons. And in order to obtain employment they go to temporary employment agencies which have job contracts that only last 4-6 weeks, which is not even enough time on the job to get unemployment benefits. Or good wages, most of those jobs pay only minimum wage. (7.25 hr.) If you're not union in the company you work for will not have a

40 hour work week instead it's 34 hours a week full-time and it's the law! Unemployment is how you can measure *"poverty creation!"*

2. Inflation—Cost of living and Recession Bubbles.

Think about what the national debt and deficit would be if we didn't have inflation? Without any controls it will very soon *cost too much to live!* Here is a couple of ideas I have,

1) End supply-side economics completely
2) A flat price law for all products and service fees. With as a guideline a national average for EA. Product and service fee with strong enforcement.
3) Make it illegal to do massive layoffs and or plant shut downs if that company is profitable if the reason is economics. The only time we should lay someone off their job is due to poor performance.
4) Abolish the Wall Street futures market.
5) Stop and repeat right to work laws!
6) The creation of jobs that pay good wages (middle class salaries and wages).

Recession—bubbles are caused do to consumer confidence which that common everyday people don't' have the money to be able to afford to purchase their products. When that happens it should be legal to have our government make them take price—cuts instead of cost of living increases or adjustments. Calling it a national economic emergency!

3). Taxes.

Well let's see! I guess a good place to begin is to examine individual tax rates.

A good question is the individual rate that I pay is the same as what corporations pay?

And the answer is because conservatives would have you believe it's the same rate but it's not. Our individual rate is call the individual marginal tax rate, which they hike that a lot!

The bush tax cuts were $750 Billion dollars lowering the individual corporate rate from 39.4% to 35% and combined with expenditures at $750 Billion Dollars. Total to be $ 1 trillion $500 Billion dollars a year from 2001 to 1012 which offset the deficit by almost $12 trillion dollars. WE need to ask former vice president Dick Cheney if deficits really matter now.

The middle class are really upset. Whom I feel deserve tax relief not rich people! And you are lucky I'm not president you're individual tax rate would be 42% until the national debt was paid back and then lover the rate to 39.4%

Well that's enough about taxes.

4). Health Care and Well Being (Retirement).

Now let's talk about the new health care law! Affordable Care Act, and yes Obama-Care!

For one thing he did not cut Medicare by $700 Billion dollars either what he did do was eliminated a $700 Billion dollar a year. Tax Subsidy that was giving to insurance companies so they could sell supplemental Medicare Policies. What I understand is Republicans want to repeat Obama-care to repeat that tax subsidy of $700 Billion a year and privatize Medicare that would severely inflate cost of insurances and the cost of all health care!

Do you remember that Obama-care chart that Republicans have used to describe the new 140 agencies to implant it!

Well none of its true!

Where they got that chart from was form a college text-book that's supposed to describe how government agencies inter-act on a daily basis. I remember that very chart from class, I use to have called state and local gout. That chart was in that textbook!

Now as far as the I.R.S with $ 16,500 new agents is because of pas budget cuts restores the agencies needs for those agents! And I can guarantee they will not be implementing Obama-Care.

5). Education.

This is another government investment you don't want to fun because it cost too much to fund through state revenue subsidies so for the last thirty three years school boards all over the country have shut school buildings down and sold them to private charter schools through school vouchers. My opinion is forget trying to spur-economic growth!

The rich will survive!

Renew state revenue subsidies without education you will not have a very stable economy!

Ask mayor of Chicago Rahm Immanuel how much a convention center cost? That answer will probably be 63 public school buildings.

6). Safety and Security.

With supply—side economics it has even put our own safety and security as risk?

You might say how? Not having enough food inspectors at the food and drug administration or inspectors or agents at the environmental protection agency. You are putting health and our food at risk, our drinking water and the air we breathe!

All because of economic freedom!

You have to grow the economy.

Security? Because of creating more poverty you want us fighting among ourselves! With more stand your ground laws with less law enforcement agencies.

7). Climate Change.

Yes! I feel it is a part of our economy. The violent storms we have had that is costing a lot to clean up, with their billion dollars costs. Let alone the droughts that cause food prices to rise.

When you could have cheaper energy-sources like wind and solar within this market may have $20 million good-paying job opportunities that it could represent especially with less violent storms and less costly cleanups.

8). Measuring Gross Domestic Product. Or (G.D.P)

Oh! Wow! I almost forgot how do they measure economic growth? By leading economic indicators unemployment rate consumer price index and gross domestic product.

Measuring gross domestic product sis measure supposedly by stock and inventories or keeping up with supply and demand but in reality it measures price increases or inflation.

9). National Debt and Deficit.

National debt at beginning of 2013

Was $17 trillion dollars but they tell me it's being paid down.

Congressional budget office has a breakdown of the debt, according to them almost $12 trillion of it was Bush tax cuts $2 trillion war in Iraq and Afghanistan.

Now were going to stop for a minute! Now think about the total debt and what it would be without inflation! I know it would not be $17 trillion dollars! There should be a time when we need to raise the debt ceiling without legislating the act of. Now you know more about the economy and just remember you can't have a decent conversation without.

Chapter Seven

STUPID STICK POLITICS

Now you are probably thinking to yourself what the hell is he talking about now? Stupid stick politics is when you have a democrat who compromises their principals and their values and act like a conservative because their worried about election or they think it's just fashionable to act like that! The stupid-stick is constantly being used in the U.S senate a lot since 2008 and here are a lot of examples: February, 2009 a letter was sent to majority leader Harry Reid about holding up presidents Obama's agenda to take a better look at it! It was signed by every moderate democrat in the senate when I saw that news segment yes! It was in the news cycle that day! So it was well documented thirty democratic senators had signed the letter right after congress passed the clean-energy bill. Which would have created a whole lot of good paying jobs.

I am thinking to myself thirty of them why. That's half of our filibuster proof majority! Within a year after that congress passed well over 430 pieces of legislation that would have really fixed the economy and gave us a better country by far. If they would have passed congressmen Henry Walkman's clean Energy-Act before they passed the affordable—care act A.K.A (Obama-Care) there would have been a different result at the 2010 elections.

It did not stop there either especially when Rahm Emanuel then chief of staff at white house when he called his former liberal colleagues in congress F XXNN! Retards for calling and complaining about how senate chairman Max Bacchus took the public option out of Obama-care!

Here are other examples of the stupid stick being played in the U.S senate look at *filibuster rules change episodes!*

Yes all that Obama over a senate rule change which I feel needs rule changes, they should be able to pass something on a simple so vote majority instead of 60 votes. And to stand and give reasons why you object to legislation being presented instead of a secret hold on the legislation being considered.

But instead of letting U.S senator Markey of Oregon of US. Brown of Ohio to present their legislation they sat while Sen. Levin of Michigan. And Sen. McCain of N.Y have a conversation about the rules change on the floor. Mitch McConnell of Kentucky at a press conference mutter the same thing he always says. Well we beat the liberals again! With a big smile! And the continuation of the drama with presidential appointments and the nuclear option in which nothing was done with either. I think it is safe to say we have a moderate controlled U.S senate and when you have that kind of control you will not either get things done or pass legislation that favors conservatives. Yes the stupid-stick! A pretty serious con-game almost like the U.S senate is still controlled by republicans with by-partisan support form moderate democrats.

Other examples is in leadership when every other day Harry Reid being for a simple so vote majority or a 60 vote majority.

My opinion is everything but an international treaties or compact and or agreements should take fifty votes to pass all other legislation like an international treaty it should take 67 votes.

Now to explain the stupid-sticks!

Republicans pass them to moderates to beat back the liberal when this is done I think poor people and middle class feel it the most out here in main street.

I am going out on a limb and say something you may not like. Hillary Rahman Clinton former senator and secretary and secretary of state use to have a job as corporate lawyer for Wal-Mart. Yes! Wal-Mart based on that job can anybody really trust her? I know I can't! As president of the United States True liberals need a better voice and to overcome the pit falls and gridlocks of the U.S senate. 67 U.S senators yes I want a super majority but you have to have better than half of 34 seats or better to have that liberal voice, other political parties like the green party to disband and to join the democratic party. Ralph Nader quit being an unreasonable man and stop telling as how conservative the Democratic Party and rejoin us and settle for being a senator or congressmen and stop the stupid-stick! And quit being a political victim of divide and conquer!

I would like to see more primary challenges in the Democratic Party just for moderates and corporatists and other conservatives.

Well now you are probably saying to yourself how you do know? How do you tell them apart?

A litmus test of two basic questions

1). Do you believe in supply-side economics? Tax cuts for job creators
2). Do you support the keystone of pipe line? More than likely they will answer yes to both questions? We cannot have candidates that compromises principles and values of the Democratic Party. And always remember if compromise principals of values they are no good for the party of the country.

Now inclosing on the subject of the stupid stick! If a candidate should compromise any *true democratic principles or democratic values they should not be a member of the Democratic Party!*

Chapter Eight

DIVIDE AND CONQUER

This is the con-game that matters most of all it's how republicans and other conservatives drive a wedge between the middle-class and the poor even the working poor gets effected. When you tell that voter how lazy we are not to work and re-dependent on the government thinking that were entitled to housing, food, you name it! And this is why the economy is so screwed up! Because the poor won't work, just like Mitt Romney said we need to be taught a better work ethic in kinder-garden! Takers! And makers! And it's also why the middle class pays more in taxes!

What do you suppose is missing in this conversation?

The fact is they were once tax payers, got laid off through no fault of their own because of economic reasons! So the C.E.O can save money! But yet these corporations make record profits and when candidates tell their voters that they're going to have to fit—it so they can keep more of their hand earned money! Which is what I call the *Great American White Lie!*

Because really do you think it can still resonate with voters after all these years? Some of them still believe it. Which is the biggest motive I have for writing this book! Because I personally have been subject to the bigotry myself.

Let alone the stuff you have done during election-years over the last 30 years by telling college students they will impound their cars, bikes and motor-cycles if they vote are make their parents pay taxes to the state that the college is in they attend.

And now you've made your former practices into voter—Id laws.

And get third party candidates on the ballot to take votes away from your opponent. But you see this what you do to get elected! You have to cheat and con to get elected because you like the power!

Chapter Nine

TO THE TAXED ENOUGH ALREADY
CROWD A.K.A TEA PARTY

The tea party is the biggest reason why we should stop and eliminate supply-side economics! Been fully funded by the Bush tax-cuts quite the job creation huh! Two different conservative philosophy factions coming together to help stop liberal socialism and take their country back!

Made up of libertarians and conservative Christians. But how I don't blame you never have but never will. Because really you don't know and don't have a clue to what is really happening to you're I know you are taxed enough already! But please stop listening to Rush Limbaugh, Sean Hannity and Fox News and you're crazy politicians and above all stop *voting against* your own *self-interests!* Have you seen the government they want! The only branches of government that they want is Dept. of defense Dept. of Justice, Supreme Court, Presidency, U.S congress and U.S Senate and that's all! Is that not the government they used to have in the Soviet Union?

If libertarians you say is a disease I don't never want to be cured! And if that's the best you got than you should just keep mouth closed and not say anything!

And as soon as you break everybody into a better work ethic! You wait till you're laid-off and have to use food stamps or other public assistance! When it happens to you, you better hope that liberals are still around otherwise you won't have any political voice at all. Especially when they point the finger at you and say that's why you're paying a lot in taxes! And when that happens you still going to blame it on diseased liberals? And in closing of this subject you also don't have clue about true patriotism.

Chapter Ten

SELF INTEREST LEGISLATIVE BENEFITS
AND OTHER ENTITLEMENT TALES

The self-interest of a conservative while their sitting in public office is astounding! I mean they sit there passing legislation that puts tax dollars in their own pockets most of the time without the tax payers even knowing about it. And when liberals want to do something for the poor and middle class they yell about control spending! Tax and spend! Tax and Spend Quit spending! The hippocras run deep! Always remember a conservative will not pass any tax credit legislations job contract, Health-care provider, tax subsidies or anything involving spending unless *yes they themselves* can get something out of it!

Examples:

The keystone XL pipeline anyone that supports passing that and trying to push the president to okay the project has investment stock in those companies involved in the construction of the pipeline. And they say it will create a lot of jobs which is probably a *con*. Because the facts say it will create 35 full-time jobs 35? Speaker John Boehner Having stock in all 8 companies involved in the construction of said pipeline. And Congressman Lamar Smith who has the most investments even in trans-Canada the main company. Even U.S sent Heidi Hide Camp moderate democrat from North Dakota! U.N Ambassador Susan Rice had investments in it yes! And she was never confirmed as secretary of state@ I think conservatives really slipped up there huh?

Speaker John Boehner pointed out to Leslie Stahl at a 60 minute interview the Sunday before Election Day of 2010 in that interview was talked a plastics company in southern Ohio that he owns said to have a four million dollar a year profits. Common sense will tell you plastic products are made out of chemicals from oil.

So could it be why they won't repeat the oils gas to subsidy is because member of congress and senate maybe putting some of that tax subsidy in their own pocket! Or congress woman Michelle Bachman with a Farm subsidy for the family farm or Medicaid health provider payments to her husband for his guidance clinic that practice prayer for therapy!

Let alone! Why do you think they don't want don't want to lift the salary cap of 106,000.00 on social security retirement benefits for its recipients? I believe they rigged it for themselves so they could receive those retirement benefits without paying payroll taxes especially president Reagan who was drawing those benefits even before he ran for president. Thus any recipient receiving retirements benefits will be paying taxes on those benefits will be paying taxes on those benefits. But all the time the legislation was signed into law in 1981 the salary cap was $ 88,000.00 per year. And gradually adjusted for inflation to where it is now at $ 106,000.00 per year.

Liberal Democrats in southern states could win in southern states by linking moderate democrat primary challenges and all other general election challenges to self-interest government spending of that type putting extra tax dollars in their pockets but in order to that show facts like their voting record on those issues and specific record of him either pocketing the money or spending it on themselves. Something like that avoids a lot of muds slinging throughout their campaigns! Like being punch in gut.

Chapter Eleven

THE FEAR FACTOR

Be very afraid!

This con-game is all about having us be afraid of Russia-China and EL-Agenda. We always have to have someone to fight as part of perpetual war, because with conservatives we always have to have a war as part of that governing make up Sharia Law in North Carolina just voted on a law that refuses to recognize Sharia Law or to make it illegal all because they think that liberal and president Obama will institute Sharia Law at the federal level! You know what I say to that, that's just plain crazy! How that law like could evoked in our country?

Conservatives have no understanding or even know what Sharia Law is. To them it's something evil that radical Islam conjured up when in fact it allows a husband and father can treat their wives and daughters any way they see it, starve them! And beat on them! And if they do things they don't like their allowed to kill them! Do you really think that for one minute we could have a law like that here in America?

Common-sense will tell you No! Not Ever! And now I want to talk about Iran developing nuclear weapons and yell how this is unacceptable! You can't pick and choose who has those weapons. If we yell about! I simply say how we can be such hypocrites about it! Especially if we are giving these weapons to other countries. And all of the fear profit scams there is. Everything from predicting the end of the world to the battle of Armageddon to the second coming of Christ. There has always been a lot of these people that make a lot of money scaring the hell out of us! To get us to vote for conservatives to keep us safe. See my next book called *Fear for Profit Scams* there will be more of an in-depth look into subject.

Chapter Twelve

SHRINK GOVERNMENT OR GROW GOVERNMENT
AND OTHER AUSTERITY TALES

Budget cuts are synominus with conservatives what I mean is they use it as a tool for governing properly to make the middle-class think that they are saving tax dollars by cutting the cost of programs and services when in fact they are not. My question is! Are they really saving you tax dollars? I say no! Because do you see a tax bill lower than the previous year?

And now for job killing regulations when regulations protect the health and safety of workers and consumers. Remember that egg processing and packaging plant in Iowa with nine foot high mountains of increments and dead rats. You really have to ask yourselves can employers and Wall Street really police themselves.

I don't think so!

Before there is a recall someone has to die or get sick from a product first! That is unacceptable.

Because why wait till something happens so why not have more food inspectors or I.R.S agents or investigators and other agents at environmental protection agency or other agencies that are supposed to be there looking out for us. So fund those agencies and quit playing games! And creating more poverty! Give us the government services we pay for! No police! No fire fighters! No school teachers! And when you finance and outsource those government positions it cost the tax payer almost three times more than it would cost to pay an employee of the government for that job.

A lot of work has to be done to restore all government services and its agencies as well as funding of those services and agencies. But it does have to done! The promise of our state and federal government to keep us safe and healthy and without those agencies and regulations they cannot keep that promise!

Remember that gulf oil spill when we had some of our conservative politicians saying accidents will happen! Well! I was always raised if you did *wrong take responsibility and pay your actions.*

Chapter Thirteen

CLOSURE

Oh my!

I am on the last chapter. I am so glad I had this time to lay out a new bold fresh perspective on the con-games of politicians play and how they rigged our system to make better financial gains for themselves and their campaign donors. Now I do have some ideas for better governance.

1. A flat price law for all products and services
2. Make it illegal for corporate officers to use the reason of economics and or economic reason to lay off their employees!

You want to do something more constructive instead of complaining and wanting to cut government programs and series because of their high price tags. Do something to control the cost of living and or inflation! Have better common sense.

Even in my home state of Michigan where supply-side economics has been invoked to create jobs what a concept! Emergency Finance managers that was passed, and then a referendum was on the ballot in the last election and was defeated and then passed again by both houses and resigned into law.

Now to finance the job creation their taxing retired senior citizens retirement pensions. Now I want to say this about the bankruptcy of the city of Detroit. Detroit has not been right since 1967 with the riots. If you can bail out corporations you should be bailing out bankrupt cities, schools, and other municipalities instead of corporations! Restore federal revenue subsidies instead of tax cuts for job creators. One of the biggest reason I wrote this is for the distance and hate that the middle class conservatives have for the poor. As I said before you want to push them to go to work then you push that rich corporate executive to hire us.

Let me remind you from 2001 to 2012 they received $ 1 trillion $500 billion dollars a year adding almost $2 trillion dollars to the national debt which their trying fix—it so that the poor and the middle-class to pay for it. Example: a letter from my congressmen telling me and reminding me that $46,500.00 is my share including my children and their children, sounds almost like a bill of a demand notice. Well I want to tell him that, that's not our bill! They tell me how you are worth $80 million dollars. Why don't you and you're relatives that own Whirlpool Corp., pay your fair share of income taxes and pay the debt down, because we are not the ones that wanted those tax cuts to create jobs or to prop up your companies with a tax subsidy.

I am not envious of rich people either! I just want them to abide by the laws of our country and be an American and patriotic and pay your fair share of taxes and take responsibility when you break a law and take the consequences.

Liberals let's have a better voice! Talk about supply-side economics ruining the country and don't be afraid of taking all this poverty that has been created and talk about your opponent socking away extra tax dollars from the tax payers, Federal Healthcare providers, tax subsidies, job contracts and talk about how they themselves benefit from those pieces of legislation involving tax dollars of the taxpayers, which would stop a lot of mudslinging! And/or playing I know you are? But what am I? Which as you know can have a devastating effect on your campaign. And always remember if your poor and in poverty, not too long ago you did pay your fair share of taxes.

And inclosing, I would like to say that the middle class taxpayers are the American people that's in desperate need of tax relief really bad so cut Marginal tax rates!